habitats
and the animals who live in them

habitats
and the animals who live in them

Anita Ganeri and Penny Arlon

weldon**owen**

weldon**owen**

Authors: Anita Ganeri and Penny Arlon

Design: Tory Gordon-Harris, Natalie Schmidt, Anna Pond

Editorial: Lydia Halliday, Susie Rae

Fact checker: Tom Jackson

Art Director: Stuart Smith

Publisher: Sue Grabham

Insight Editions Publisher: Raoul Goff

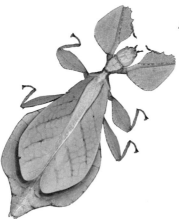

Published by Weldon Owen Children's Books

An imprint of Weldon Owen International, L.P.

A subsidiary of Insight International, L.P.

PO Box 3088
San Rafael, CA 94912

www.insighteditions.com

ISBN: 978-1-68188-742-5

Manufactured in China

First printed 2020

24 23 22 21 20 1 2 3 4 5

Contents

Look for the fun activities in each chapter. There are mazes, dot to dots, word searches, sticker scenes, and more!

Find the giant poster and sticker sheets at the end of the book!

Hello Habitats

From the highest mountains to the deepest parts of the sea, animals live all over the world. You can find them in scorching deserts, steamy rainforests, rushing rivers, and even at the icy ends of the Earth. The places that animals live in, and that provide them with food and shelter, are called habitats, and there are many different types. Some are hot and dry; others are cold and wet. Some teem with trees and plants; others are barren and bare. Habitats can be very large, such as an ocean or grasslands, or on a much smaller scale, such as a rock pool, or a single leaf on a tree.

Animals often have to adapt or change so that they can survive in their particular habitat. They have special features to help them. Animals that live in the sea often have bodies that are streamlined for swimming, and may also have flippers or fins. Animals that live in deserts are adapted to survive in the heat, and have special ways of finding water, even when it doesn't rain for weeks on end. Thick fur, feathers, or fat help animals at the icy poles to stay warm. Many animals are suited to life in one place, and may not be able to live in any other habitat or survive if their habitat changes.

In this book, you will meet animals from many different habitats, from wonderfully colored fish on a coral reef, to great herds of zebra and wildebeest roaming the grasslands. See if you can work out how they are adapted to life in their particular home.

Beach

A beach is an ever-changing habitat where land and sea meet. Beaches can be sandy or rocky, creating plenty of space for animals and birds to live and feed. But they are also challenging places to live in. They change shape constantly as the waves and wind wear them away, and, twice a day, the sea rises and falls on the beach, as the tides go in and out. Shoreline creatures must find ways of coping with being soaked by sea water, then being left high and dry.

Tern

Sea snail

Lobster

Seagull

Pelican

Cormorant

Parakeet

Ticks

Kelp fly

Land snail

Crawfish

Baby sea turtle

Spider crab

Sand dollar

Whelk

Puffin

Clams

Curlew

Sea lion

Sandpiper

Scallops

Snow plovers

Humboldt penguins

Anenome

Shore crab

Jellyfish

Blue swimmer crab

Abalone

Conch

Sea stars

Shrimp

Sea urchin

Limpets

Caiman

Lugworm

Swan mussel

Brittle star

Sand hopper

Hermit crab

Red land crab

Iguana

Goose barnacles

Rockskipper fish

Jellyfish

Atlantic horseshoe crab

Sea anemone

Sea snail

Killdeer

Sea louse

Ark clams

Siamese crocodile

Dalmatian pelican

Mosquito

Shore crab

Little ringed plover

Crayfish

Short-tailed shearwatert

Saltwater crocodile

Blue-footed booby

Crab

Mussels

Blue soldier crabs

Sea slug

Cockles

Limpet shells

Sea urchins

Clams

Kellen's whelk

Sea stars

Fairy penguin

Portuguese Man O War

Sea urchin

Razor Clams

Abalones

Marine crab

Flamingo tongue snail

Pied cormorant

Common Tern

Atlantic puffin

European cormorant

Nautilus

European sanderling

Oysters

Winkles

Whelk

Ghost crab

Great cormorant

American oystercatcher

Zebra mussel

Lobster

Seagull

Eurasian oystercatcher

Barnacles

13

On the beach

Head to the the beach to solve these puzzles. What will you find hiding in the sand and swimming in the rock pools?

Find the chicks

Follow the lines to help the birds find their chicks.

SHELL HOME

The hermit crab is born without a shell. It climbs inside an old shell left by another animal!

Maze

The baby turtle needs to find its way to the sea. Can you help?

start

finish

Word search

Find the beach creatures hidden in the word grid.

c	r	a	b	s
l	m	o	p	h
a	d	f	v	e
m	g	u	l	l
s	n	a	i	l

Gull

Crab

Snail

Clam

Shell

Mountains

With soaring slopes and snow-capped peaks, mountains can be perilous places. The higher you go, the colder and windier it gets and the thinner the air, making it harder to breathe. The slopes are sometimes bare and rocky; sometimes icy or covered in snow. Despite these harsh conditions, many animals make their homes on mountains. They soar and glide on the thermal winds rising above the peaks, clamber and climb up the rocky slopes, and take shelter in warm, underground burrows to avoid the worst of the winter time.

Takin

Muskrat

Goral

Black bear

Marmot

Ants

Alpacas

Japanese snow monkey

American bald eagle

Mountain wolf snake

Ribbed pine borer beetle

Cougar

Mountain ringlet butterfly

Hercules beetle

Dragonfly

Giant panda cub

Mosquito

Snowy plover

Red panda

Mountain nyala

Monal pheasant

Gray wolf

Cicada

Honeybees

Chamois

Pill bugs

Trout

Ticks

Wild goat

Mandrill

American beaver

Alpine chough

Andean cock-of-the-rock

Centipede

Bullseye giant silk moth butterfly

Boreal owl

Tibetan Macaque

Giant anteater

Snowcock

Ibex

Simien wolf

Barbary sheep

Snow leopard

Western diamondback rattlesnake

Andean condor

Yellow jacket wasp

Coyote

Apollo butterfly

Common raven

Longhorn beetle

Grasshopper

Reindeer

Moose

Llama

Monarch butterflies

Spectacled bear

Mountain kingsnake

Bhutan glory

Lynx

Walia ibex

Wild yak

Black widow spider

Rosy boa

Salmon

Pika

Painted lady butterfly

White-tailed deer

Brown bear

Golden orb spider

Mountain hare

Toucan

Gorilla

Markhor

Gelada baboon

Kea

Mouflon

Up the mountain

Wrap up warm to climb the snow-peaked mountain. Can you spot any animals with super-furry coats?

Sticker scene

Look for the eagles on your sticker sheet. Add them to the mountain scene.

Use your stickers here!

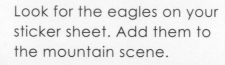

A WARM COAT

The yak has such long hair that it almost reaches the ground! It keeps the yak super-warm during the freezing winter.

Matching pair

Can you find two llamas that are exactly the same?

What comes next?

Look at the animal patterns. Can you work out which mountain animal comes next on each line?

Use your stickers here!

Rainforest

A thick blanket of lush, green forest grows around the steamy equator, which is the rainforests of our world. It is hot, wet and humid all year round in the rainforest, providing ideal conditions for animals to live in, with plenty of food to eat and places for breeding and shelter. In fact, rainforests are home to millions of plants and animals—more than anywhere else on Earth. They live in every layer of the forest, from the towering tops of the tallest trees, to the dark and gloom of the forest floor.

Fer-de-lance

Great hornbill

Tree kangaroo

Tiger beetle

Piranha

Resplendent quetzal

Spectacled owl

Jaguar

Giant anteater

Red-eyed tree frog

Tamandua

Leafcutter ants

Poison arrow frog

Orangutan

Sugar glider

Macaw

Okapi

Lowland gorilla

Sloth

Tailless whip spider/scorpion

Iguana

Civit

Howler monkey

Morpho butterfly

Jewel beetle

Sunbird

Oropendolas

Mandrill

Amazon kingfisher

Capybara

Fishing spider

Red ibis

Forest elephant

Tarsier monkey

Baby black caiman

Jumping spider

Toucan

Harpy Eagle

Yellow-headed caracara

Tapir

Anaconda

Nine-banded armadillo

Australian king parrot

Mosquito

Bat

Capuchin monkey

Ulysses butterfly

Scarlet macaw

Tiger

Blue and gold macaw

Gibbon

Common tree shrew

Cairns birdwing

Scorpion

Leopard

Stag beetle

Click beetle

Lemur

Ticks

Hyacinth macaw

Jaguarundi

Emerald tree
boa constrictor

Spider
monkey

Army ant

Buffon's
macaw

Coati

King
vulture

Binturong

Rhino beetle

Ocelot

Pangolin

Javan
rhinoceros

Amazon
parrot

Black panther

Jabiru
stork

Heliconius

Chimpanzee

Tarantula

Giant
rainforest
mantis

Loris

Green-winged
macaw

Longhorn
beetle

In the rainforest

Hike through the rainforest to solve these puzzles. The rainforest is filled with animals, but they are sometimes hard to find!

Can you find?

Can you find two frogs, three spiders, four butterflies, and five ants?

FOREST GARDENER

Forest elephants are very important to the rainforest. They eat lots of fruit, spreading the seeds in their poop so that the seeds grow into new trees!

Odd one out

Which red-eyed tree frog does not have a matching twin?

Color me in

Rainforest birds can be super-bright! Use lots of different colors for this parrot.

Shadow search

The jaguar is searching for its dinner. Look at the shadow! Which animal has it found?

Anaconda

Monkey

Armadillo

Capybara

Tapir

Follow the lines

Which frog will catch the cricket? Follow the lines to find out.

SPEEDY SWINGER

The spider monkey is the king of the swingers. It moves from tree to tree swinging by its hands, feet, and tail!

Draw the other half

Can you draw the other half of the rainforest beetles?

Jewel beetle

Goliath beetle

Odd one out

There are six toucans flying over the rainforest. Which one doesn't match the others?

33

Ocean

Vast stretches of salty sea water cover around
two thirds of the Earth. This lies in five oceans—the
Pacific, Atlantic, Indian, Southern, and Arctic.
Together, they form the largest habitat on Earth.
As you descend into the oceans, there are many
different zones of life, from the vast expanses of
the open ocean, to the freezing, blackness of the
deep. These zones are home to a huge variety
of animals, from microscopic zooplankton to
gigantic blue whales, the largest animals that
have ever lived.

Baby harp seal

Lobster

Scallop

Skate

Clymene dolphin

Giant triton

Hammerhead shark

Pygmy blue whale

Banded sea krait

Queen conch

Barracuda

Humpback whale

Ribbon eel

Stonefish

Atlantic cod

Sea lion

Goby

Electric eel

Flamingo tongue snail

Guitarfish

Shrimp

Hawksbill turtle

Crayfish

Whale shark

Manta ray

Longfin spotted snake

Sea lion

Jellyfish

Nautilus

Sea slug

Scampi

Bonnethead shark

Flying fish

Marbled stingray

Portuguese Man O War

Squid

Sailfish

Pufferfish

Flounder

Long-spine porcupinefish

Tiger shrimp

Blacktip reef shark

Seahorse

Blue-ringed octopus

Bottlenose dolphins

Dolphinfish

Beluga whale

Albacore tuna

Grouper

Bigeye fish

John dory

Moray eel

Walrus

Leafy sea dragon

Basking shark

Beluga sturgeon

Orca

Salmon

Wolffish

Trumpetfish

Bluefin
tuna

Narwhal

Sardines

Moray
eel

Blue marlin

Manatee

Red
hump fish

Hermit crab

Deep-sea
angler fish

Krill

Octopus

Red
snapper

Green
turtle

Squid

Manta ray

Honeycomb
moray eel

Gray reef
shark

Geoduck
clam

Dugong

Under the ocean

It's a big, big ocean out there. Take a deep breath and dive into these watery puzzles!

How many left?

The hungry sharks are racing toward the fish. Will they get one each?

PLAYTIME!

Dolphins love to play with each other. They squeak and whistle, leap out of the water, and butt heads!

Sticker scene

How many sea lions can you find on your sticker sheet? Fill the kelp forest with sea lions!

Use your stickers here!

Odd one out

Look closely at the seahorses. Which one doesn't have a curly tail?

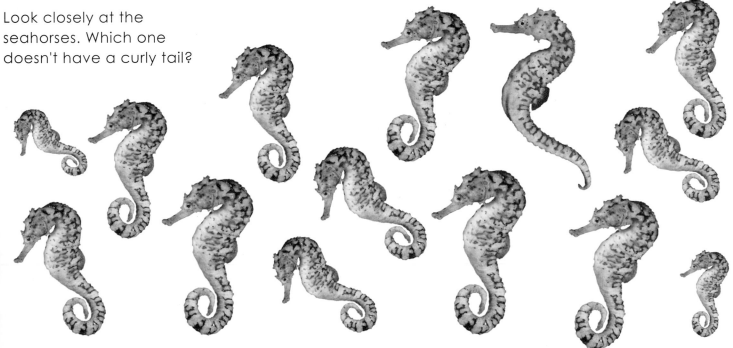

Polar

At the furthest ends of the Earth lie the coldest places on our planet—the Arctic and Antarctic, also known as the Poles. Here, it is always freezing cold and windy, and ice covers large parts of the land and sea. Polar animals are experts at survival. Polar bears, which are only found in the Arctic, have thick fur coats to keep them warm, and hairy feet that grip the slippery ice. Penguins, which are only found in the Antarctic, have thick, waterproof feathers that keep them warm and dry as they swim. In the icy ocean, some fish have chemicals in their blood that stop their bodies from freezing solid. In this section, we look firstly at animals that live in the Arctic, followed by those in Antarctica.

Arctic

Orca whale

Cod

Skua

Vole

Narwhal

Ground shrew

Lynx

Viviparous lizard

Gyrfalcon

Arctic ground squirrel

Caribou

Moor frog

Great gray owl

Arctic fox

Baby harp seal

Bald eagle

Moose

Walrus

Marmot

Woolly bear caterpillar

Lemming

Beluga whale

Dall sheep

Damselfly

Wood frog

Arctic tern

Polar bear

Snowy owl

Siberian husky

Canada goose

Arctic hare

Arctic char

Bearded seal

Ptarmigan

Red fox

Musk ox

Snow goose

Wolverine

Arctic wolf

Puffin

Barnacle goose

Roe deer

Antarctic

Krill

King
penguins

Albatross

Crabeater
seal

Gentoo
penguin

Adelie
Penguin

King
crab

Antarctic
petrel

Weddell
Seal

Antarctic
Toothfish

Humpback
whale

King
penguin

Southern
elephant seal

Giant
petrel

Weddell Seals

Lantern fish

Snowy sheathbill

Antarctic fur seal

Chinstrap penguin

Sea stars

Antarctic springtail

Humboldt penguins

Orca whale

Wandering albatros

Short-tailed Shearwater

Trumpetfish

Crabeater seal

Sperm whale

Imperial shag

Ocellated icefish

Leopard seal

In the snow

Brrrr! It's cold at the poles, so don't hang around! How quickly can you speed through these chilly puzzles?

Maze

The reindeer are lost. Help them to find their way back to the herd.

start

finish

CUTE CUBS

A polar bear mom almost always gives birth to two babies. The cubs live with their mom for up to three years.

Dot to dot

Connect the dots, starting at the number 1. Who will you find?

Odd one out

Look carefully at the penguin chicks. Which one doesn't match the others?

What comes next

Can you work out which polar animal comes next on each line?

Use your stickers here!

Desert

Rolling seas of sand, or vast, rocky wastes, deserts are one of the world's most hostile habitats. Temperatures can range from baking hot during the day, to freezing cold at night, and sometimes no rain falls for years and years. It seems remarkable that animals can live in such inhospitable places, but they have many features to help them keep cool and find enough water. Some, like camels, can go for days without drinking. Others, like gerbils, shelter from the daytime heat in cool burrows underground.

Sidewinder

Scarab beetle

Fennec fox

Gila monster

Gemsbok

Vinegaroon

Spotted hyena

Armadillo

Bactrian camel

Crab spider

Centipede

Blister beetle

Tarantula

Bearded dragon

Black-tailed jackrabbit

Ball python

Greater earless lizard

Darkling beetle

Pronghorn

Elf owl

Baboon

Gerbil

California kingsnake

Ants

Rock hyrax

Desert iguana

Scorpion

Desert horned lizard

Ostrich

Lappet-faced vulture

Sonoran desert toad

Black widow spider

African wild dog cubs

Addax

Gray's monitor

Western scrub jay

Locust

Jerusalem cricket

Rosy boa

Bat

Great roadrunner

53

Hummingbird

Ringtail

Ankole
longhorn
cattle

Sun spider

Caracal

Dingo

Indian
wild
asses

Checkered
beetle

African pygmy
hedgehog

Aardvark

Thorny devil

Coyote

Longhorn
beetle

Chinkara/Indian gazelle

Spadefoot
toad

Chuckwalla

Damselfly

Desert tortoise

Burrowing
owl

Desert bighorn
sheep

Dromedary camel

Praying mantis

Bilby

Arabian oryx

Kangaroo rat

Australian spider beetle

African crested porcupine

Cicada

Rattlesnake

Armadillo lizard

Gila woodpecker

Cactus wren

Assassin bug

Black-footed cat

Burchells sandgrouse

Meerkat

Honeybee

In the desert

Phew, it's hot in the desert! Solve these puzzles and discover which animals live in the heat.

Matching pairs

Pair up these desert lizards. Which one does not have a matching twin?

SUNBATHERS

Meerkats live in tunnels that they dig under the desert sand. In the mornings they climb out to sunbathe and warm up.

Help the camel

The camel is trying to find the water hole. Which line should it take?

Word search

Can you find the desert animals in the word grid?

p o w l g
s n a k e
t m n j c
w a t l k
f o x r o

Gecko

Ant

Owl

Snake

Fox

Grassland

Huge, dusty plains of grass grow around the world. Few plants can grow in grasslands —the soil is too sandy and dry for many plants to grow, apart from tough grasses and a few, scattered trees. In Africa, huge herds of animals—zebras, antelope, giraffes, and elephants—graze the grasslands and gather at the rare waterholes. They are preyed on by grassland hunters, such as lions, leopards, and hyenas. Above them soar bare-headed vultures, on the look out for scraps.

Wall brown
butterfly

Zebra

Jaguar

Leopard
tortoise

Ants

Helmeted
guineafowl

Meerkat

Grasshopper

Dung
beetle

Ferret

Cheetah

Egyptian cobra

White-
backed
vulture

Komodo
dragon

Giant anteater

Termites

Hyena

Lion

Lion
cub

Common
blue
butterfly

Caracal

Hoopoe

Dhole

60

Serval

Skipper butterfly

Springbok

Puff adder

African elephant

Grey crowned crane

Gaur

Black-backed jackel

Bush dog

Chameleon

Mole

Klipspinger

Hartebeest

Joey

Red kangaroo

Weaver bird

Barn owl

Pheasant

Locust

Leopard gecko

Ball
Python

Ostrich

Impala

Red-tailed
hawk

Thomson's
gazelle

American bison

Black
mamba

Grasshopper
sparrow

Vervet
monkey

Horse

Aardvark

Baboon
spider

Nyala

Prairie
dog

Vulturine
guineafowl

Leopard

Egyptian
vulture

Bumblebee

Wildebeest

Giraffe

Warthog

Mosquito

Griffon
vulture

Greater
kudu

Opossum

Black
rhinoceros

Firefly

Ticks

Guanaco

White
rhinoceros

Ants

Tiger

White lion

Emu

Fox

Buffalo

Simien wolf

On safari

It's time to head out into the grassland to spot some of the biggest, tallest, and fastest animals on Earth!

Sticker scene

Can you find the elephants on your sticker sheet? Add them to the grassland scene.

Use your stickers here!

SPEEDY CAT

The cheetah is the fastest running land animal in the world. It can run at full speed for about a minute.

How many left?

Count the nests and the birds. Are there enough nests for each weaver bird?

Find the shadows

Look at the shapes carefully. Can you match the animals to their shadows?

Can you find?

Look at the grassland animals. Can you find four tortoises, three butterflies, two birds, and one snake?

PRIDE OF LIONS

Lions live in families called prides. You can spot a male lion because it has a furry mane around its head.

Matching pair

Can you find two antelopes
that are exactly the same?

Color me in

Which colors will you choose
for these dung beetles? Make
them nice and bright!

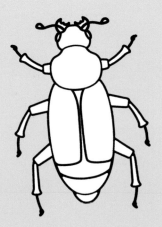

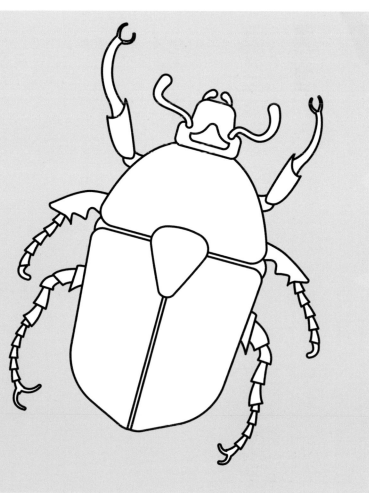

Rivers and Lakes

Starting off as a stream high up on a mountainside, a river flows downhill, fast at first, then slowing down as it reaches the sea, and its journey ends. On its way, it wears away waterfalls, scrapes away valleys, and fills lakes. Animals swim and feed underwater, or shelter in the plants that grow along the river bank. Many animals spend part of their lives in water, and part on land. Lakes are also home to hundreds of animals, including huge flocks of brightly-colored flamingoes on some African lakes.

Hippopotamus

Blue-spotted
salamander

Fish
eagle

Snake-head
fish

Penguin
tetra

River crab

Coypu

Green
anaconda

Axolotl

Flamingos

Trout

Mandarin
duck

Red
discus fish

Stork

Black-
crowned
night
heron

Blue
discus fish

Dragonfly
larvae

Amazon river dolphin

Fish eggs

Piranha

Leech

Fishing spider

Crocodile

Beaver

Scarlet ibis

Mayfly

Water snake

American Bullfrog

Crayfish

Walleye

Dalmatian pelican

Southern leopard frog

Red lechwe

Otter

Alligator snapping turtle

Pike

Water beetle

Coot

Monarch butterflies

Fishing owl

Giant snakehead fish

Carp

Damselfly

Albino American alligator

Stickleback

Fire Salamander

Salmon

Betta

Tadpole

Mosquito

Mallard duck

Duck-billed platypus

Eel

Barbel

Waterbuck

Zooplankton

Oscar fish

Kingfisher

Neon tetra

Spoonbill

Alpine newt

Black swan

Egret

Baikal seal

Koi carp

Red-eared slider

Ducklings

Manatee

Backswimmer

Catfish

River snail

River dolphin

Hydra

Sturgeon

Osprey

Water shrew

Toad

Freshwater prawn

Vole

River mussels

Water scorpion

Pike perch

Yellow perch

Alligator

White swan

Canada Goose

Lapwing

Clown featherback

European cormorant

Loon

African jewelfish

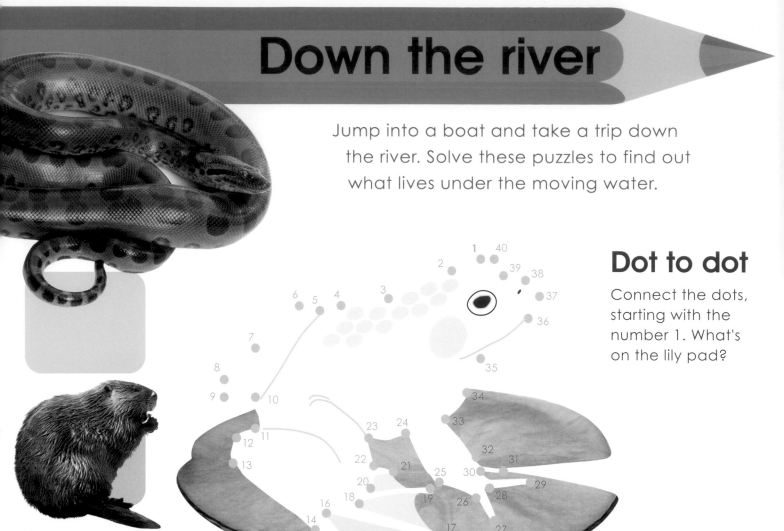

Down the river

Jump into a boat and take a trip down the river. Solve these puzzles to find out what lives under the moving water.

Dot to dot

Connect the dots, starting with the number 1. What's on the lily pad?

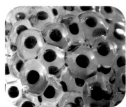

Matching pair

Look at the turtles. Can you find the matching pair?

PINK DOLPHIN

Most dolphins live in the ocean, but not this one! The pink river dolphin lives in the Amazon River.

Shadow search

Can you match the river animals to their shadows?

Maze

The kingfisher wants to dive for fish. Can you help it find its way to the river?

start

finish

75

On the lake

There are lots of animals to spot on a lake. But keep watch! The lake may look calm, but danger lurks beneath.

Follow the lines

The otters are hunting for the crayfish. Which one will find it?

SNAP!

Watch out for the Nile crocodile as it hunts in the lake. All you can see is its eyes, ears, and nostrils above the water.

Matching pair

Look at the long-legged flamingos. Can you find the matching pair?

What comes next?

Look at the animal patterns. Can you work out which lake animal comes next on each line?

Use your stickers here!

Woodland

A carpet of bluebells under the shady trunks of trees, a woodland is a magical place. From pine forests to beech woods, they are home to hundreds of animals. Insects scurry among the leaf litter, while rabbits make their burrows between the tree roots. Birds nest on branches and in knot holes, while squirrels scamper up and down the tree trunks. Larger animals, such as deer and bears, roam the forest floor. All rely on the trees for food and shelter, and protection from creatures higher up the food chain.

Fire salamander

Brimstone butterfly

Smooth snake

Ferret

Brown bear

Crowned sifaka

Wolf spider

Termite

Blue tit

Slow worm

Lemur

Long-eared owl

Comma butterfly

Kudu

Hedgehog

Sika deer

Tasmanian devil

Porcupine

Honeybees

Black bear

Banana slug

Bumblebee

Beaver

White rhinoceros

Horsefly

Tree frog

Corn snake

Bat

Adder

Moose

Wood ants

Hairstreak butterfly

Map butterfly

Red squirrel

Woodboring beetles

Turtle dove

Common lizard

Wolverine

Wood pigeon

Ticks

Earthworm

Eagle owl

Green tiger beetle

White admiral butterfly

Deer

Ermine

Ladybird

Racoon

Red-bellied wood-pecker

Goat moth

Woodlouse

Fox

Orb weaver spider

Reindeer

Striped skunk

Woodlouse spider

Garden spider

Grey squirrel

Purple emporor

Bee eater

Gatekeeper butterfly

Burnet moth

Mole

Grass snake

Barbary ground squirrel

Cardinal beetle

Kookaburra

Silver-washed fritillary

Badger

Wild boar

Elk

Death watch beetle

Caterpillar

Orange tip butterfly

Wasp

Caribou

Gypsy moth

Tamarin

Mink

Opossum

Chipmunk

Speckled wood butterfly

Baboon

Hummingbird

Peacock butterfly

Black grouse

Crab spider

Longhorn beetle

Soldier beetle

Koala

Pine marten

Dragonfly

Wolf

Ringlet butterflies

Devil's coach horse beetle

In the woods

Shhh. Woodland creatures are shy. Try to keep quiet while you work through these puzzles.

Sticker scene

Can you find the flying owls on your sticker sheet? Add them to the woodland scene.

Use your stickers here!

A PANDA'S LIFE

Pandas live in bamboo forests and love to eat bamboo. In fact, bamboo is about the only thing the pandas eat. They eat it all day!

Odd one out

Look carefully at the skunks. Which one doesn't match the others?

Word search

Can you find the woodland creatures in the word grid?

p	m	s	t	m
b	o	a	r	o
a	l	h	n	t
t	e	i	x	h
m	d	e	e	r

Moth

Bat

Deer

Boar

Mole

Reefs

Like a beautiful underwater garden, a coral reef
is a stunning habitat that bursts with color and life.
Fish in coats of vibrant colors dart between corals
in the shape of antlers, daisies, mushrooms, and
even brains. They swim in large shoals for safety.
Octopuses and sea snakes hide in nooks and
crannies, while giant, blue-lipped clams sit on the
sea floor. Reefs are rich feeding grounds for lurking
reef sharks, and rare sea turtles. And, once the
daytime creatures go to sleep, a community of
night-time animals take over.

Lyretail hogfish

Knifefish

Lion's mane jellyfish

Black pomfret

Purple Anthias

Spiny dogfish

Butterfish

Talang queenfish

Blackside hawkfish

Leopard shark

Grey reef shark

Bengal sergeant

Clownfish

Leopard coral grouper

Bottlenose dolphins

Mahi mahi

Mandarin fish

Brain coral

Shrimp

Kuhl's maskray

Sea urchin

Suckerfish

Frogfish

Flatworm

Blenny

Red sea bream

Striped eel catfish

Hawksbill turtle

Small-spotted catshark

Grouper fish

Coral

Pygmy seahorse

Sprat fish

Sea slug

Maldivian Lyretail

Staghorn coral

Purple firefish

Angelfish

Flounder

Giant barrel sponge

Blue-ringed octopus

Sea slug

Purple tang

Goatfish

Toadfish

Large-toothed cardinalfish

Unicornfish

Long-spine porcupinefish

Rabbitfish

Demoiselle

Saddleback clownfish

Whale shark

Blue-spotted stingray

Anenome

Butterflyfish

Crown of thorns starfish

Hermit crab

Yellowtail fusilier

Perch

Squirrelfish

Soldierfish

Scorpionfish

Longfin spotted snake-eel

Sea cucumbers

Pipefish

Barracuda

Parrot fish

Jewel fairy basslet

Coralfish

Sea anemone

Sea goldie

Silver biddy

Spotted sweetlips

Barred soapfish

Seahorse

Yellowtail scad

Banggai cardinalfish

Reef octopus

Grunter fish

Coral polyps

Spider crab

Pigfish

Diamond trevally

Coral hind

Seaperch

Sea anemone

Trumpetfish

Zebra cling fish

Batfish

Butterfly fish

Banded sea krait

Striped surgeonfish

Mangrove red snapper

Harlequin sweetlips

Moray eel

Stonefish

Tripletail

Garfish

Razorfish

Clown triggerfish

Murena spotted eel

Giant clam

Lionfish

Wrasse

Bannerfish

Red gurnard

Redfin velvetfish

On the reef

The coral reef is very colorful.
Look at all the spotted, striped,
multi-colored sea creatures.
But watch out for the hungry shark!

Matching pair

Look at the reef fish. Can you spot two that are exactly the same?

CORAL HOME

Coral reefs are home to
many sea creatures.
In fact a quarter of all
types of sea creatures
live on or around
the reefs!

Color me in

Use blues, greens, and yellows to brighten up this octopus.

Spot the difference

Can you find two differences between these sea slugs?

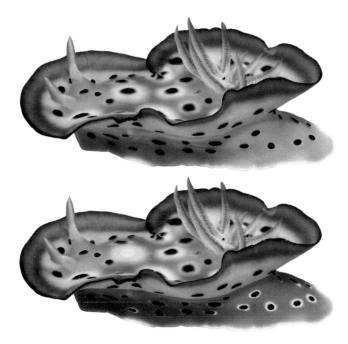

Maze

The clown fish is searching for somewhere to hide. Help it reach the anemone.

start

finish

Which way home?

The parrot fish wants to find its way home to the reef. Which line should it take?

Draw the other half

Can you draw the other half of the jellyfish?

DON'T EAT ME!

The lionfish is very beautiful but very dangerous. It has poisonous and deadly spines. Other fish don't try to eat it!

Count the legs

Count the arms
and legs. Which reef
animal has the most?

Shadow match

The reef shark is hunting. Match
the shadow to see which sea
creature it is chasing.

Stingray

Starfish

Squid

Turtle

Urban

The hustle and bustle of a city might seem an unlikely place to find animals. But parks, gardens, and city buildings have become a valuable habitat for wildlife. Many animals move to the city because their natural habitat is under threat. The city offers them plenty of places to shelter, and rich pickings of food, often from trash cans and garbage. Animals quickly adapt to their new surroundings. Instead of trees, birds nest in chimneys and roof eaves, or in nesting boxes in people's gardens.

Rabbit

Python

Rooster

Mosquito

Hamster

Ferret

Mallard
duck

Red
squirrel

Cockatoo

Chicks

Moth

Lizard

Pigeon

Zebra
angelfish

Sphynx cat

Tarantula

Labrador
retriever
puppy

African
grey parrot

Koi fish

French
bulldog

Weimaraner

Seagull

Ladybug

Parakeet

Goat

Sheep

Butterflies

Shrew

Scorpion

Cat

Bats

Crow

Racoon

Ducklings

Locust

Garden snail

Chow chow

Telescope goldfish

Fox

Skunk

Lovebirds

Mallard duck

Bumblebee

Termites

Chicken

Toad

Piglets

Quails

Goldfish

Chipmunk

Cockroach

Corn snake

Housefly

Peacock

Iguana

Gecko

Guinea pig

Mute swan

Green turtle

Parrot

Silkworm

Gerbil

Owl

Ants

Rats

English bulldog

Turkey

Gray squirrel

Dalmatian puppy

Brahman calf

Mouse

House spider

Red setter

Hedgehog

Flea

Aphids

Maltese

Hare

Slug

Wasp

Cricket

Pony

Siamese cat

Chicken

Garden spider

Dove

Common lizard

Earthworm

Ticks

Grasshopper

Common kestrel

Goose

Siberian husky puppy

Canary

Tortoise

House moth

Honeybee

Cow

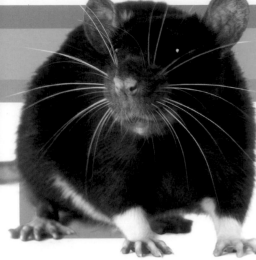

In the city

Step into the city to see all sorts of pets and wild animals. There are more animals living with us than you might think!

Follow the lines

Follow the lines to help the animals find their babies.

CITY SINGERS

City foxes live in family groups. They can jump over high garden fences and often make their dens in garden sheds.

Matching pair

Look at the six kittens. Can you find the matching pair?

Word search

Find the town animals in the word grid.

Bee

p	d	t	c	b
m	o	u	s	e
h	g	w	l	e
c	a	t	r	u
k	d	o	v	e

Dog

Dove

Cat

Mouse

Camouflage

Now you see it. Now you don't. Some animals have adapted to their habitats in clever ways. They have special colors or patterns to help them blend into their surroundings, so that they stay safe from hungry predators. In the rainforest, some animals, such as insects, are disguised as the leaves they feed on. In the deserts, some lizards match the stony ground. Some animals, such as this snake, use their cunning camouflage to sneak up on their prey without being seen. Its unfortunate victim will not spot it, until it's too late.

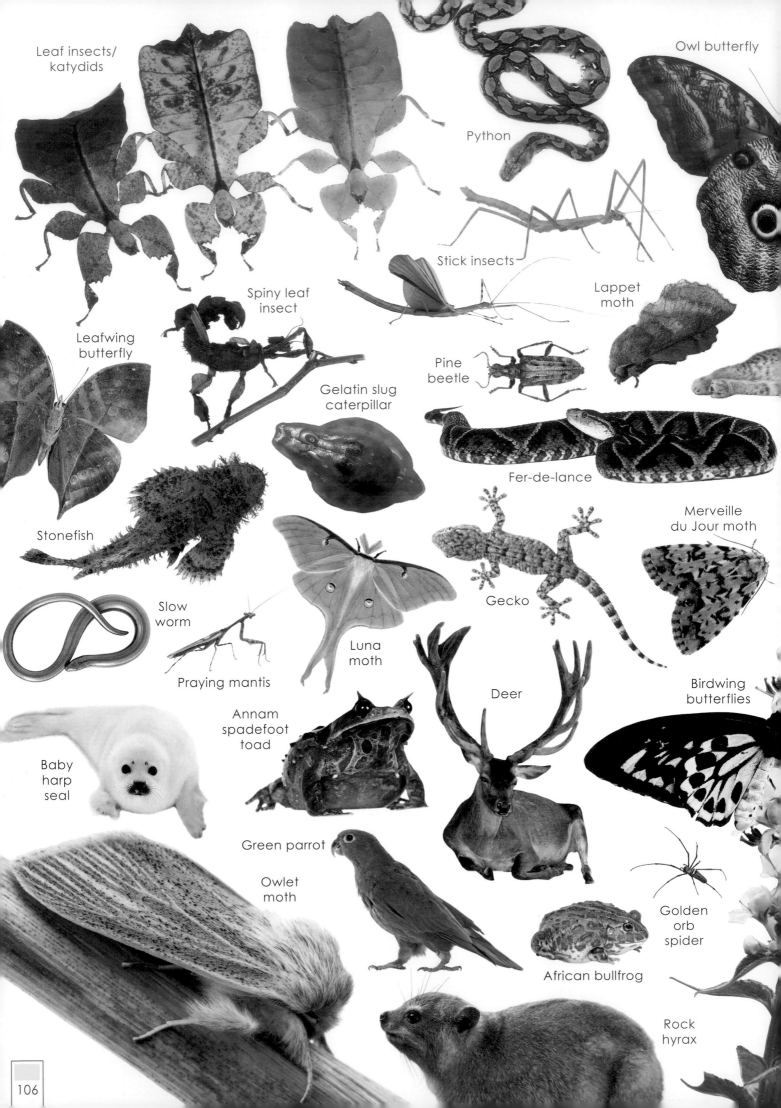

Leaf insects/ katydids

Python

Owl butterfly

Stick insects

Lappet moth

Spiny leaf insect

Leafwing butterfly

Pine beetle

Gelatin slug caterpillar

Stonefish

Fer-de-lance

Merveille du Jour moth

Gecko

Slow worm

Luna moth

Birdwing butterflies

Praying mantis

Deer

Baby harp seal

Annam spadefoot toad

Green parrot

Owlet moth

African bullfrog

Golden orb spider

Rock hyrax

Chameleon

Ticks

Earthworm

Arctic fox

Locust

Lynx

Orchid mantis

Lunar thorn moth

Ball python

Rhino beetle

Puff adder

Snowy sheathbill

Koala

Lion

Fox

Leopard

Lime hawk moth

Anole

Gray tree frog

Woodcock

Caterpillar

Chrysalis

Sidewinder

Bearded dragon

Red-eyed tree frog

Grass snake

Crab spider

Quail

Sword-grass Moth

Tawny frogmouth

Green tiger beetle

Flounder fish

Wood ants

Polar bear

Lizard

Moray eel

Aphids

Scorpion

Desert horned lizard

Wolf spider

Hedgehog

Mountain hare

Hermit crab

Gila monster

Mossy frog

Burrowing owl

Green lacewing

Garden snail

Woolly bear caterpillar

Cuttlefish

Leaf-tailed gecko

Kudu

Red squirrel

Leafhopper Larva

Green tree python

Cheetah

Barnacles

Grasshopper

Spider

Porcupine

Giant peacock moth

Toad

Leafy sea dragon

Stink bug

Dock bug

Scorpion fish

Iguana

Rattlesnake

Reef octopus

Camouflage

You'll have to look carefully to solve these puzzles. These animals know how to hide!

Maze

The bush cricket is trying to reach the leaves. Can you help it reach them?

start

finish

HIDE AND SEEK

Even a big animal can hide against its background. This giraffe is the same color as the grassland and can be difficult to spot.

Can you find?

Each animal is hiding in the picture below it. Can you spot each one?

Snake

Moth

Stick insect

Frog

Jaguar

Sticker scene

Look on your sticker sheet. Can you find any animals that could hide in this scene?

Use your stickers here!

111

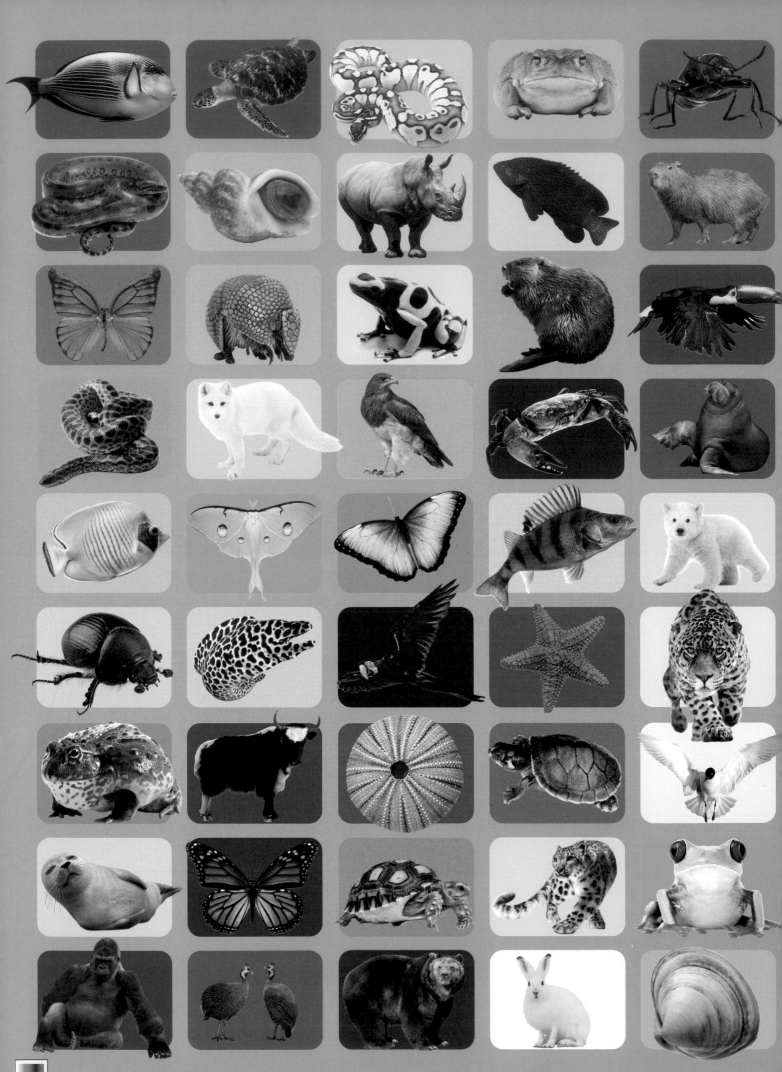